MAYSOON ZAYID,
The Girl Who Can Can

MUSLIM MAVERICKS

Vol. 1

MAYSOON ZAYID, The Girl Who Can Can

Dr. Seema Yasmin

Illustrated by Noha Habaieb

New York Amsterdam/Antwerp London
Toronto Sydney/Melbourne New Delhi

An imprint of Simon & Schuster Children's Publishing Division
1230 Avenue of the Americas, New York, New York 10020

Cover design by Laura Eckes

For information about special discounts for bulk purchases, please contact Simon & Schuster Special Sales at 1-866-506-1949 or business@simonandschuster.com.
Simon & Schuster strongly believes in freedom of expression and stands against censorship in all its forms. For more information, visit BooksBelong.com.
The Simon & Schuster Speakers Bureau can bring authors to your live event. For more information or to book an event, contact the Simon & Schuster Speakers Bureau at 1-866-248-3049 or visit our website at www.simonspeakers.com.
Also available in a Salaam Reads hardcover edition
Interior design by Sammy Yuen and Marigold Kitzmiller
The text for this book was set in Bodoni Egyptian Pro.
The illustrations for this book were rendered digitally in Procreate.
Manufactured in the United States of America
1225 BID
First Salaam Reads paperback edition February 2026
2 4 6 8 10 9 7 5 3 1
Library of Congress Cataloging-in-Publication Data
Names: Yasmin, Seema, 1982- author | Habaieb, Noha illustrator
Title: Maysoon Zayid, the girl who can can / by Seema Yasmin ; illustrated Noha Habaieb.
Description: First Salaam Reads hardcover edition. | New York : Salaam Reads, 2026. | Series: Muslim mavericks ; volume 1 | Audience: Ages 6–10 | Audience: Grades 2–3 | Summary: "This is the story of the girl who could! Maysoon Zayid was just a girl from New Jersey. She might have been the youngest of four sisters, but in her dreams, she was Mimi—an amazing actress, comedian, and dancer! The only problem? People kept telling Maysoon that she could not live out her dreams. As a Palestinian Muslim girl born with cerebral palsy, Maysoon faced all sorts of challenges—both physical and societal—that stood in the way of her goals. But Maysoon didn't dare give up! Instead, she followed her heart all the way to the screen and stage to become one of America's first ever Muslim women comedians and an actress on her favorite TV show"—Provided by publisher.
Identifiers: LCCN 2025012645 (print) | LCCN 2025012646 (ebook)
ISBN 9781665953429 (hc) | ISBN 9781665953412 (pbk) | ISBN 9781665953436 (ebook)
Subjects: LCSH: Zayid, Maysoon—Juvenile literature | Actors—United States—Biography—Juvenile literature | Comedians—United States—Biography—Juvenile literature | LCGFT: Biographies
Classification: LCC PN2287.Z38 Y37 2026 (print) | LCC PN2287.Z38 (ebook) | DDC 791.4302/8092—dc23/eng/20250513
LC record available at https://lccn.loc.gov/2025012645
LC ebook record available at https://lccn.loc.gov/2025012646.

For all the girls who were told they
were too much and not enough
—S. Y.

To my precious Nadine and Elias:
You're the ones who can
—N. H.

PROLOGUE

Who are you in your wildest dreams? Are you an astronaut jetting to the moon in a spaceship? Are you a scientist discovering the cure for cancer? Are you a dancer on Broadway, the world's best teacher, or the inventor of a machine for time travel?

Maysoon Zayid was just a girl from New Jersey with three big sisters and a couch for a bed[1]. But in her dreams, in her hugest, wildest, most delicious dreams, she was Mimi. Mimi was an actress, comedian, dancer, and the first Muslim

---

[1] It's not like Maysoon didn't have her own bed. But if she slept on the couch, she could avoid her sister's loud music *and* she could watch TV while everyone else was asleep.

girl to win every major acting award: an Oscar, a Golden Globe, an Emmy, and a Tony. Winner, winner, winner. What a dream!

Maysoon dreamed of singing, dancing, and acting her way into the hearts of millions. She dreamed of being an entertainer. Have you seen the Hollywood sign in California? The one high up in the hills with the big white letters? That's how big she wanted her name to shine!

She wanted it lit up for the whole world to see: **MAYSOON ZAYID, better known as MIMI: winner of all the awards on the planet for best entertainer.**

There was just one problem with Maysoon's dream. Something stood in the way of it coming true.

1

A GIRL WITH BIG DREAMS

One sunny morning in September, Maysoon woke up on the couch that she called her bed, stretched her arms, and smiled. She felt tiny bubbles of excitement fizz up from her toes, through her belly, and all the way up to her head. Today was the day! Finally she was old enough to join her three big sisters at Public School Number Six in her hometown of Cliffside Park, New Jersey.

Lamiah, Feda, and Hanan loved school and the many friends they had made there. Every day they came home from school and told Maysoon stories of the games they had played (that was mostly Feda), the fun they had had (that was mostly Hanan), and the boys who they liked (that was mostly Lamiah).

Maysoon was excited to strut her stuff through the playground, wearing her favorite pink pants with the bells at the bottom. She was ready to wave to her sisters in the food hall and to make new friends and tell them about her love of soap operas and her dreams of becoming the best entertainer in the world. "And the

Academy Award goes to . . . Maysoon 'Mimi' Zayid!" She needed to tell her new friends that one day they would hear these exact words. Maysoon would be one of the world's best-loved entertainers.

Maysoon's mom worked long hours in a hospital laboratory. It was her dad's job to drive Maysoon to school to get enrolled. Maysoon smiled and bounced in her seat for the whole drive.

But when they arrived at the school, a teacher said four words that shattered Maysoon's dream. "She can't come here," the teacher said. Maysoon's dad was in the middle of writing Maysoon's name on the list. He lifted his head and frowned.

Maysoon's mouth opened wide. She gasped. ***What?! How can this teacher*** *say I can't come to this school? This teacher doesn't even know me!*

Before Maysoon could say a word, her father dropped his pen and spoke in a loud voice. "My daughter is brilliant! Let her in or I will sue!" he said, jabbing the air with his finger.

"Yeah! We'll sue!" Maysoon said. "I'm good enough for this school! Why can't I go with Lamiah, Feda, and Hanan? Why can't I make friends with their friends? Why do I have to go to a different school?"

The teacher pushed his glasses up his nose and crossed his arms. He whispered to Maysoon's dad as if Maysoon weren't there. "This girl is different," the teacher said. "You'll have to speak to the superintendent about her."

Maysoon's dream began to melt. It became a puddle of stinky glop that turned into a nightmare. A nightmare in which Maysoon's dream of becoming an entertainer would surely fail. How could she become the world's best entertainer if she couldn't even get into the school of her choosing?

2

TOO BOLD, TOO MUCH, TOO DIFFERENT

There was something that made Maysoon different from her sisters and from many children in their school. But being different is not bad. It's just . . . different. Differences make us unique. Differences can mean that some of us need extra help—help with things like walking, talking, or learning.

The thing that makes Maysoon different happened to her when she was a baby. When she was being born, the doctor made a mistake. Instead of a smooth entrance into the world, she was stuck for a while, maybe for a few minutes. The doctor didn't help her make it out into the world in time.

Being stuck meant that she didn't have oxygen—and brains need lots of oxygen. When her brain didn't have oxygen for those crucial first minutes, it was hurt. Messages that went from her brain to her muscles became jumbled. Because of that, her muscles don't always behave like she wants them to.

This is called cerebral palsy, CP for short. ***Cerebral*** means to do with the brain. ***Palsy*** means "weakness." Maysoon isn't the only girl with CP. Every single year in America, ten thousand babies are born with CP. It is the most common cause of disability in American children.

Across the whole world, there are

seventeen million people with CP. That's almost as many people as there are in the whole of New York State. When Maysoon learned how many babies are born with CP, she thought, ***I guess I'm special, but not that special!***

CP made Maysoon shake, shake, shake. Almost like she was dancing without trying. Sometimes CP made it hard for her to swallow food. Sometimes CP made it hard for her to talk, causing her to slur her words. CP made it hard for her to walk in a straight line, so when she was a little girl, Maysoon's dad would put her feet on top of his shoes, hold her hands in his, and walk across the room. He encouraged her to walk by saying "Yes, you can can!"

Not everyone with CP shakes or

cracks jokes and makes people laugh or walks or slurs their speech or dreams of making it big as an entertainer in Hollywood. Some people with CP can't walk without the help of a walker. Some have to use a wheelchair, and while Maysoon sometimes struggled with her words, some people with CP can't talk at all. Meanwhile, others with CP have no problem talking nonstop! A group of ten people might all have CP, but CP can look different for each of them.

Differences make us unique. Differences shouldn't divide us. But Maysoon was about to find out that not everyone understands what being different means. Other people's misunderstandings were about to get in the way of her big dreams.

3

THE GIRL WHO WOULDN'T BE TOLD NO

So, back to school. Back to the teacher saying that Maysoon—teller of jokes, lover of television, and future Oscar, Golden Globe, Emmy, and Tony Award winner—could not go to Public School Number Six. Because she was different. Because she had CP.

Maysoon's dad marched straight into the superintendent's office to prove that Maysoon was amazing and that she could attend the same school as her big sisters.

"Come in!" The booming voice hit Maysoon's ears before she had even walked into the superintendent's office. "Enterrrr!"

Maysoon looked at her dad. Her dad looked at her. ***Right!*** she thought. ***Let's***

get in that office and show the school superintendent that he is wrong! Doesn't he know that disabled girls can be smart and strong and funny? Maysoon put her feet on top of her dad's feet, gripped his hands tightly, and marched into the office.

Look! she wanted to say. ***Look at me! I can walk!***

Maysoon hopped up and down on her dad's feet. She didn't say what she was thinking out loud. Instead, she showed the superintendent that with the right kind of help, she could walk into his office and prove that he was wrong, that differences were okay. ***Don't judge people before you meet them!*** That was what she wanted to say.

The superintendent was tall. Even

taller than Maysoon's dad. He looked like Abraham Lincoln. "Well, hello," he said. "How are you?"

Maysoon wanted to flick her hair and roll her big brown eyes at him. Instead, she took a seat and said she was fine. That was when the superintendent walked over to her and said he needed to test her. He towered over Maysoon and barked orders. "Count to ten!"

And because Maysoon was clever and independent and knew so many numbers, she broke the rules. ***I'll show him***, she thought. Instead of counting to ten, she counted to one hundred! If she had wanted to, she could have counted to ten thousand.

The superintendent didn't like that. Maysoon hadn't followed the rules. To make matters worse, in between counting to one hundred, which was so easy for her, she spoke to her dad in Arabic, the language they spoke at home.

The superintendent narrowed his eyes. He hovered over Maysoon. He arched his eyebrows and flared his nostrils. He looked at Maysoon's dad and said, "I'm sorry, but we still won't be able to accommodate her."

Maysoon's dad argued with the superintendent. "But look at how smart she is!"

The superintendent argued back. "She belongs in a school for children with Down syndrome," he said.

Some babies are born with Down syndrome. People with Down syndrome can have problems with their hearts or difficulties learning. Some children with Down syndrome go to schools for children like them who have Down syndrome. Some go to schools that are for all kinds of children.

Maysoon didn't have Down syndrome. She had a different disability. What was important to her was being able to choose where she went to school. It was her dream to go to the same school as her big sisters.

The superintendent looked at Maysoon and shook his head. He leaned in toward Maysoon's dad. "She's too different for this school."

He was talking about Maysoon as if she weren't there! Maysoon looked at the superintendent's face. She could see in his eyes that he believed deep down that

Maysoon belonged in a different kind of school.

There's nothing wrong with going to a school designed for children with disabilities. Just like there's nothing wrong with using a wheelchair or a walker to help you get around. But Maysoon did not like that the superintendent had decided where she should go to school without getting to know her first. She didn't like that he was making up his mind without seeing what she could and couldn't do. Without knowing that CP made her muscles hurt all the time. Without knowing that she loved to sing and dance and act and make people laugh. He didn't know that Maysoon listened to comedy shows at home to teach herself how to tell dazzling jokes—jokes that would one day make people pee their pants.

The superintendent had heard that Maysoon had CP and didn't understand that everyone with CP is not the same. Everyone is different! Maysoon felt that she should get to choose where she went to school. And she had decided: She wanted to go to the same school as her big sisters.

Maysoon's dad explained this to the superintendent. The more her dad explained, the more the superintendent listened. And the more the superintendent listened, the more his face changed. His nostrils were less flared. His eyebrows less arched. He even uncrossed his arms. Maybe . . . Was he . . . ? Could he be . . . changing his mind? Could Maysoon's dream of attending the same school as her big sisters become a reality?

The superintendent leaned over Maysoon. His face was so close to hers that she could smell the coffee on his breath. *What will he say? Will he say*

yes? she wondered. *Or will he say no? I think he'll say no. But I don't want to go to the other school! I want to go to the same school as—*

"I have decided that Maysoon can attend this school."

"YESSSS!" Maysoon punched the air. Her dad laughed as Maysoon hopped up and down on his shoes. Maysoon was one step closer to her dream of becoming an entertainer, because if this wish of attending the same school as her sisters was possible, then Hollywood, her name in bright lights, crowds of screaming fans, and bucketloads of fan mail were in her future too.

Maysoon laughed and smiled and sang her favorite songs all the way home. She couldn't wait to tell her mom and her big sisters that she would soon be singing and twirling through the hallways of their school—of her dream school.

But Maysoon didn't know that a bigger challenge was yet to come. Something else was about to get in the way of her big dream.

4

HERITAGE AND HOPE

In a world that said disabled kids should be treated differently, where did Maysoon find the strength to speak up for herself in the superintendent's office? Why was she bold enough to count to one hundred when she had been asked to count only to ten? In a world that said it was rude to speak Arabic in front of a school superintendent who only spoke English, why did Maysoon feel confident speaking another language with her dad? Where did her inner strength come from?

Maysoon's mom and dad were born in a village called Deir Dibwan in Palestine, thousands of miles from Maysoon's home in New Jersey. Her dad's dad was a shepherd, and her dad's mom had many babies. Some of those babies died. Nine of them survived.

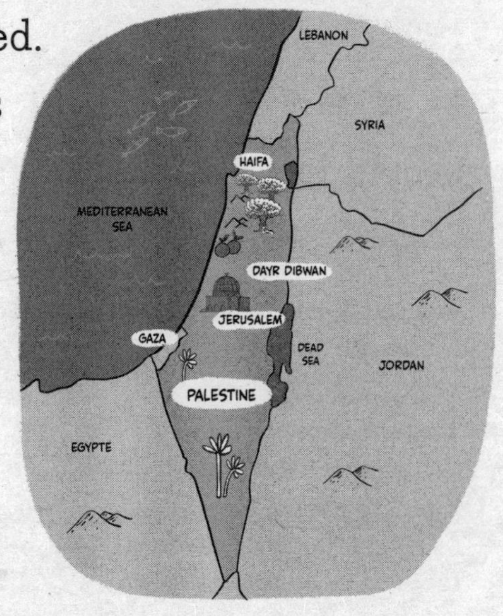

There was rarely enough food for her dad and his brothers and sisters. Each night, her dad prayed there would be enough meat on the table to feed so many hungry mouths. He was used to going to bed with an aching stomach and a heavy heart.

Maysoon's parents told her stories about Palestine. They told her how the Palestinian people had suffered pain and hardship for a long time. Their homes and lands had been taken from them. Precious fields filled with ancient olive trees had been burned. But even though life was hard and things were taken and destroyed, the Palestinian people never gave up hope, her parents said.

They rebuilt their homes. They planted new trees. They cooked great feasts and invited all the neighbors. They told their stories to give one another hope when times were tough. And they always dreamed. Dreamed of being free, of picking juicy olives and flying colorful kites in the sky with friends.

In Maysoon's case, she dreamed of

seeing her face on the big screen and her name in bright lights. She

dreamed of stardom and a life as an entertainer, a life of movies, Broadway, and standing ovations.

Why did Maysoon dare to dream so big? Why did she believe that a Palestinian American girl from New Jersey who shakes, shakes, shakes with CP would make it all the way to Hollywood? When Maysoon thought about her visits to Deir Dibwan, when she remembered the stories of her dad going to bed with an empty stomach, she wondered: *Is this where I get my strength—from my Palestinian family? From our heritage? Did I inherit hope and a never-quit attitude from my ancestors who have been through so much?*

Maysoon asked herself these questions on her trips to Palestine. Every summer, her parents sent Maysoon and her sisters far away from New Jersey. The girls packed their bags, got on a plane, and flew thousands of miles east to visit their grandparents in Deir Dibwan.

One hot day in the village, Maysoon and her sisters were sitting in their grandmother's house feeling bored in the heat. Suddenly, Feda looked around the room and pouted. ***Uh-oh***, Maysoon thought. ***Feda's about to start trouble!*** Feda stared at each of her sisters and asked a daring question. "Who is your favorite sister?" she said. "You can pick only one." What a cheeky question!

The sisters sat and thought for a while. Maysoon pointed at Feda. Feda pointed at their eldest sister, Lamiah. Hanan pointed at Lamiah. Nobody pointed at Maysoon. Maysoon was mad and confused. She put her hands on her

hips and pouted. ***But*** I'm ***the cute one!*** she thought. ***How can nobody pick me?***

Maysoon knew things wouldn't always go her way. Just because she had gotten into the same school as her big sisters, just because she was funny and kind and had lots of friends, didn't mean she was used to getting all the things she wanted. But she ***was*** used to being treated fairly. At home her mom treated her and her sisters as individuals. They were each treated with respect and kindness. That didn't mean they were treated exactly the same or were expected to do the same things as everybody else. And that was okay, because everybody is different.

Maysoon's mom taught her that even if things seem to not be going her way, she should hold on to her dreams and remember that dreams are worth the hard work. “Sometimes, when you want something, you have to work really hard to get it,” her mom would say.

Take physical therapy, for example. Physical therapy is exercises, stretches, and movements that help people keep their bodies healthy, especially their muscles and bones. Because Maysoon had CP, physical therapy was important. Working with a physical therapist to do lots of stretches and exercises would help her control her muscles better. Maysoon found all the stretching and the weight lifting to be hard work. Sometimes it felt boring, and it always took up too much time.

Not only was physical therapy sometimes boring and annoying, but it was also expensive. Maysoon's parents couldn't afford a physical therapist. But that didn't stop Maysoon from stretching and flexing her muscles and working to improve her flexibility and balance. Every single morning her dad would wake her up a whole two hours before it was time to go to school, and they would exercise together. Her dad became her physical therapist!

Maysoon would lie on her back and bicycle her legs in the air. She would touch her finger to her nose and then touch her dad's finger.

Back and forth. She would walk on his feet, up and down the room. "Yes, you can can!" her dad would say, cheering her on as she walked and yawned in the early morning.

Maysoon's favorite way to work her muscles was to dancercise—that's dancing and exercising at the same time. She loved to show off her dance moves. Not having PT couldn't put a dampener on her dancing dreams! Whether she was in the village in Palestine or at home in New Jersey, whether she was the favorite sister or not, she

let everybody know that she had the best dance moves.

While her dad was amazing at doing physical therapy with Maysoon, her mom worried about her missing out on professional help. Her parents put their heads together and hatched a plan. They came up with a clever solution . . . a cheaper solution! They would enroll Maysoon in dance classes.

When Maysoon heard the news, she jumped with joy and twirled with delight. "This is the best news ever!" she said, jumping up and down. Since her dream was to become an entertainer, and entertainers needed to know how to boogie, why not start dance classes now? She couldn't wait to wear a tutu and make shapes on the stage.

But Maysoon was about to get a lesson in something more painful than messing up dance moves in front of a big crowd.

5

FIND ANOTHER DREAM?

Teri's School of Dance was named after the mother of Maysoon's best friend who owned the dance studio. Maysoon liked Teri, but she was truly in love with another dance teacher, Dawn. Dawn was dazzling enough to be a Broadway star but spent her afternoons teaching Maysoon how to pirouette like a ballerina and kick her legs high like the Rockettes.

Maysoon twirled and smiled and bounced around that dance studio as if she were on Broadway. Because that was where she wanted to be: doing the cancan on the big stage. When she danced, her dad cheered and clapped! Maysoon could see his mouth moving even though she couldn't hear him over the music. Her dad was saying: "Come on, Maysoon! You can do it! Yes, you can can!"

Maysoon was so good at dance that she was picked to attend a special dance convention in Manhattan. "Listen up!" she announced at dinnertime one night. "This is a very big deal. I am going to New York City to train with actual, true-to-life Broadway dancers!"

Maysoon's family was excited. Her dad drove her to the theater in Manhattan. The lights were bright, and the names of the stars were in huge letters on a banner above the theater doors, exactly where she dreamed her name would shine one day.

On their first morning, the teacher had all the dancers stand in a line and say their names and their biggest dream. The teacher smiled and nodded as one by one, each young dancer opened their hearts and shared their ambitions. When it was Maysoon's turn, she stepped forward and announced, "My name is Maysoon Zayid. They call me Mimi, and my dream is to be an entertainer! One day I will tap-dance in one of the biggest shows on Broadway!"

The teacher didn't smile at Maysoon's dream. They didn't clap or nod their head like they had when everybody else had shared their future hopes. Instead, the teacher looked at Maysoon and pouted their lips. "Honey," they said as they crossed their arms. "You are ***disabled.***" The dance teacher didn't stop there. They called Maysoon a word that she

didn't like, a cruel word that's used to make fun of disabled people.

The teacher looked Maysoon up and down and shook their head. "Find another dream," they said. "Next!"

Just like that, the teacher crushed Maysoon's hopes for her future.

Next, Maysoon tried out for the cheer team. She danced and kicked and shook the pom-poms. But it wasn't only the pom-poms that were shaking. Her whole body was shaking. That's what happens when you have CP. The cheer captain didn't know anything about CP, and she didn't appreciate the extra moves. "Next!" she yelled. Maysoon was rejected.

While her dad's motto was "Yes, you can can!" Maysoon's mom had a different mantra. "No one can do ***everything***, but you have to try. If you fail, you fail, but try your hardest," she would say. When Maysoon cried because she didn't make it onto the cheer squad, her mom said, "But that's life, Maysoon. No one gets what they want all of the time."

That's the same thing her mom had said when she made Maysoon cut her hair short, even though Maysoon wanted to grow her hair long, like a princess. It's the same thing she said when she put a plate of rice in front of Maysoon knowing very well that Maysoon had requested spaghetti.

Life is filled with getting some of the things you want and not getting others. But Maysoon's mom reminded her to never quit. "Keep your eyes on your goal and don't give up," she said.

So even though the dance teacher told her to "find another dream," she knew that she should ignore that terrible advice. ***If you have a dream, then that's your dream. Hold on to it. You don't need to look for a different one,*** she thought.

In her final year at Teri's School of Dance, Maysoon prepared for her last dance, a big showcase of dancers who would give their best performances to stun the crowd. Maysoon practiced for months. On the big day, she danced a ballet solo to the song "Wind Beneath

My Wings." She wore a long white dress that lifted and spun like flower petals through the air as she twirled and pirouetted across the big stage.

The crowd ate it up. They cheered and clapped and even rose from their chairs to give her a standing ovation, just like she had dreamed! Girls ran to the stage and handed her flowers. Maysoon felt like a real-life star. She was on cloud nine. Maysoon was transforming into the entertainer she had dreamed of becoming. She felt content and thrilled to have all eyes on her, cheering her on and enjoying her moves.

But there was a catch. Things weren't as they seemed. Maysoon's stomach ached as she came to see what was really going on.

"Wow!" "OMG!" the other dancers whispered.

Maysoon heard their words as she walked offstage in her flowing white

dress. That was when she began to understand what they really meant when they were clapping for her.

"It's so nice they let ***her*** dance at the end."

"Yeah, she's, like, so ***inspirational***," the voices whispered.

Maysoon's heart sank. Calling someone inspirational can be a compliment. It can also be patronizing, a way of saying you feel sorry for them because you think you're better than them, that their version of good isn't as good as yours.

"It's so nice that we all clapped for the dancing ***disabled*** ballerina," one girl said.

"I'm just so glad that's not me," said another girl.

6

THE GIRL WHO REFUSED TO GIVE UP

What do you do when your dreams are crushed? What do you say when people tread on your dreams as if your dreams are weeds? Do you let your dream fade away like a distant memory? Do you hang on to your dream like your future depends on it?

The whispered words crushed Maysoon's spirit as much as they crushed her dream. The words hurt her stomach and made her heart break. They were words, but they felt like arrows piercing her soft skin. It was as if the girls had struck her with sharp stones that made her weep.

Words matter. Words can pierce and wound. Words can make a person doubt themself or not like themself. Words can make a person give up on their dreams.

Maysoon had been mocked and pitied, ridiculed and patronized. She ran to her sisters and told them: "I ***will*** achieve my dream of becoming an entertainer! I'm going to be an actress, a comedian, and a dancer! One day I'm going to act on *General Hospital*!"

General Hospital was a popular daytime television show watched by millions of people across America. People watched that show religiously. Maysoon imagined that girls just like her tuned in across the country and watched *General Hospital*, their eyes glued to the screen.

She *ooh*ed and *ahhh*ed as she was swept away by the stories on the drama. In the morning, while doing exercises with her dad, Maysoon talked about *General*

Hospital. At school, while coloring in a picture with her friend, she told them that one day she would star on *General Hospital*. After school she watched the show. At night she dreamed about her starring role on *General Hospital*, a dream she kept alive for years and years.

When it was time to go to college, Maysoon packed her bags and her dreams and took them to Arizona State University, where she would study drama and dance. She didn't want to be called "inspirational" just for living her life, and she didn't want anyone to feel sorry for her. So she chose to keep her CP a secret. Maysoon didn't tell a single classmate about her disability.

One afternoon Maysoon was in the drama studio painting a backdrop for a new play. Her classmate Cory was helping her build the set. Cory watched as Maysoon painted. She watched her arms and hands shaking every now and again. Cory put down her paintbrush and cleared her throat. "Hey, Maysoon? Why do you twitch like that?"

"I don't twitch!" Maysoon said.

"I knew it!" Cori yelled, jumping up. "You're faking it because you want people to notice you!"

Maysoon thought for a moment. She *did* want people to notice her. She just didn't want them to notice her for shaking. She wanted them to notice her because her acting made them cry and her jokes made them laugh till they cried. She tried to hide the shaking, but some days it was impossible.

Maysoon auditioned to study acting with a teacher called Jean. Jean was pretty but very scary. Maysoon had rehearsed day and night to ace her lines. The morning of the audition, she took a deep breath, stepped onto the stage, and acted her heart out. Maysoon finished and bowed. She waited for applause.

"Neeeext!" Jean yelled.

Maysoon opened her mouth in surprise. "Wait!" she said. "Wasn't I amazing?"

"No," Jean said. "Your body can't do all the things I need an actor to do. It will always hold you back."

Maysoon's lips quivered. She walked off the stage. Yet another teacher was crushing her dreams. But Maysoon knew that not all teachers were dream crushers. Some would support her dream, even supercharge it! She just needed to find the right teacher, someone who could see her talents and determination. Someone who was willing to give her a chance.

Not long after that dreadful day with Jean, a new acting teacher arrived in town. Marshall was fresh from New York City and said he was ready to pick ten lucky students to take under his wing. Maysoon auditioned for Marshall as brilliantly as she had auditioned for Jean. This time the answer was a resounding "Yes!" Marshall saw Maysoon's brilliance.

Marshall introduced Maysoon to a friend who he said could help her become a professional actor. Marshall's friend Tanya trained actors, even actors who worked on ***General Hospital***! It was thanks to Tanya and the friends Maysoon made through Tanya's classes that Maysoon began inching closer and closer toward her dream of becoming a professional entertainer.

One of Tanya's students was a girl named Terri. She had blond hair and blue eyes and was already acting on a television show. Terri convinced her bosses on the show to invite Maysoon to be an extra.

Maysoon found herself on a real-life set of an actual soap opera playing the silent role of Diner Number Three. Only the back of her head was on camera. But she didn't care that people watching at home wouldn't see her face. She didn't even care that she was silent and didn't have any lines of dialogue. She happily sat in the pretend restaurant with her back to the camera and drank it all in. Wow, it was happening! She was on a television show! Her dreams were starting to come true!

Her next big break was as a seat filler at a huge television award ceremony called the Emmys. A seat filler sits in a chair when the superstar actor who was sitting there has to get up to use the bathroom. The job of the seat filler is to make sure the audience looks nice and full and that there are no empty chairs. Some people look down on seat fillers, but Maysoon was excited to be at the Emmys! She *ooh*ed and *ahh*ed as her favorite actors strutted past in their dazzling gowns.

After the award ceremony, Maysoon went to the after-party and smiled at all the celebrities. She was sure she was the only Palestinian girl there, the only Muslim girl there, the only disabled girl there, and possibly the only person from New Jersey. One thing she did know was that there weren't many girls like her on TV; maybe there were none at all. She had never seen a Muslim actor with a disability on TV or in the movies. There were certainly no girls like Maysoon cracking jokes onstage in comedy clubs, which is exactly where her acting teacher said she needed to go next.

On her first day in comedy school, the teacher, Mike, said, "Hey, Maysoon? Why are you shaking?"

"I have cerebral palsy," Maysoon said, quickly and quietly, not wanting to talk about her disability. By this point she had stopped trying to hide that she had CP. She fully embraced it. But that didn't mean she wanted people to bring it up all the time. She was at comedy school to make jokes! She wanted to make people laugh, not tell them about the problems she had controlling her muscles or the pain she felt in her legs.

"You have to tell the audience you have CP," Mike said. "If you don't tell your audience why you're shaking, they'll wonder what's going on and they won't concentrate on your jokes." Maysoon bowed her head. She wasn't ashamed of her disability. She didn't want to talk about it either.

She was proud of all that she was and all that she had achieved. But she wanted to tell jokes about being Palestinian and Muslim and from New Jersey. She didn't want to tell jokes about CP.

But Mike was the expert and Maysoon was the student. She listened to what Mike said, and she soon realized he had a point. CP was part of her life. There were millions of people out there with CP, and not many disabled comedians or actors talking about it. Taking Mike's advice, Maysoon began her life as a stand-up comic by saying these words at the beginning of her set: "Hi! My name is Maysoon Zayid. I'm Palestinian, Muslim,

I have cerebral palsy, and I live in New Jersey!"

Crowds have loved Maysoon ever since her first days in a comedy club. One time she made someone laugh so hard they had to run to the toilet because they were about to pee their pants! Using her brain to concoct side-splitting jokes and performing onstage in sold-out comedy clubs made Maysoon feel content and thrilled.

But there was still the matter of her wildest dream. She couldn't give up on her dream of acting on *General Hospital*.

7

AND . . . ACTION!

Some people crush dreams. Some people champion dreams. Some people come into our lives to say, "Yes, you can!" (Or in the case of Maysoon's dad: "Yes, you can can.") After years of rehearsing and auditioning and dancing and hearing "Next!" and "No!" Maysoon received the biggest call of her life. She could hardly believe it. Maysoon "Mimi" Zayid had been invited to meet the boss of the longest-running and most successful TV show in American history.

You already guessed it . . . The show was *General Hospital*. The boss was called Frank, and he wanted to meet Maysoon.

Maysoon shook with excitement! This was the show she had watched religiously as a child. The show she had pictured herself starring in time and time again. The show she had told her sisters and friends that she would most definitely act in one day.

Maysoon was over the moon. She picked out her clothes and rehearsed what she would say. She knew she would blow Frank away with her charm, charisma, and talent. She was ready to knock him off his feet so he would hire her on the spot to star as an actress in *General Hospital*! Wow. Her dreams were coming true!

But then Maysoon felt a sudden knot in her stomach. A flood of memories crashed over her like an icy-cold wave. The hurtful words people had whispered or said to her face over the years came flooding back and poured over her like stinky, sticky goop.

Find another dream.

Honey, you're disabled.

Your body will always get in the way.

Oh my God. Aren't you glad you're not her?

Maysoon wrapped her arms around

her waist. She took deep breaths. Then she put her hands on her hips and told herself: ***I can do this. I really can can do this!*** Instead of thinking about the hurtful words, the dream-crushing teachers, and the cruel people she had endured, Maysoon focused on the positive things she had seen and the helpful and encouraging words she had heard.

She thought about the things that were said by kind people. She told herself: ***Maysoon, you have a meeting***

with Frank, and you will be an actress on General Hospital*!* Then she walked into the famous studio with her head held high.

The walls of the studio were lined with photos of the legends that Maysoon and millions of Americans watched on their TV screens. When Maysoon walked into Frank's office, he said five words that made Maysoon wonder if she was dreaming. Frank said: "Welcome to *General Hospital*, Maysoon." Then he told her that he wanted her on the show. Maysoon would play Zahra, a lawyer who would have many scenes over many episodes.

Her whole life had led up to this moment. All the dance recitals, cheerleading tryouts, acting auditions, and comedy classes. How many times had she heard "You're too shaky." "You're not the right fit." "You can't do

this!" "Your body will always hold you back." Maysoon had been rejected so many times that she had forgotten about all the times she had heard "Yes!" and "Yes, you can can!"

She had forgotten how tightly she had held on to her dream for fear of it being snatched away.

Now here she was. On the set of an iconic show, script in hand, ***her*** name in bright lights. The makeup artist brushed her eyelids with sparkly purple eyeshadow. The hairstylist preened her

hair until it was shiny and bouncy.

Maysoon looked in the mirror and asked herself this question: "Who are you in your wildest dreams? Are you an astronaut jetting to the moon in a spaceship? Are you a scientist discovering the cure for cancer? Are you a dancer on Broadway, the world's best teacher, or the inventor of a machine for time travel?

"This is who I am," she said to the mirror. "I am Maysoon 'Mimi' Zayid, a girl from New Jersey with three big sisters who used to have a couch for a bed. And here I am now, a dreamer of dreams; a champion of hope; a Palestinian, Muslim, and disabled entertainer; accomplisher of all I have seen in my wildest dreams."

ACKNOWLEDGMENTS

Deep and eternal gratitude to Lilly Ghahremani, who helped conjure the Muslim Mavericks series and continues to make my wildest literary dreams come true. Big thanks to Deeba Zargarpur for her careful shepherding of this series. And thank you to Maysoon Zayid for being a star, an icon, a comedic genius, and for reminding us that there is nothing more dazzling and revolutionary than a girl who speaks her truth.